Starting A Business

How to Start A Daycare Business

By Margaret Partee

Did you know that anyone can start a business no matter how old or young you are? Did you know that you don't have to have a job just to make it out here in this place we call world? Did you know that you can be anything that you want to be? You just got to have faith and believe that God will make it happen. Plus you have to work on it day by day. If you're not working towards your goal God isn't going to send you in the right direction. True, everyone has to work but not all their lives.

IF you have goals and dreams. Be sure to put

them in black and white; meaning put it on paper. If it's in black and white you can see it. Everyday it can be used as a reminder. If it's not on paper;but it's in your mind. It's like, you know what you want to do and how to do it. You just not doing it. That's when you become a procrastinator. You can procrastinate if you want. You going to look up and see so much of your life has passed you by. And so much has happened that really could have been avoided. If!!! I'm going to say it again IF!!! You would've started working on your dreams and goals you could have been there by now. I don't know what it is that you want to do. But I do know if you don't start now you will never get started. Then your goals and dreams will have only been thoughts.I bet you stuck Living a life you don't want to live. You working a job that you hate? Do you feel like your life is over? They don't teach us about business, self-employment, retirement, mutual funds,& etc in school. They teach us how to go to college. They teach us to go in debt. They encourage us to work a minimum wage paying job. They promote fancy houses and cars that we cannot afford. Just so we can live over our means and stress. Can anyone explain to me?; Why do you need so much education to get a job and basically get bossed around For thirty or forty years of your life just be told when you can retire. Or should I say? Live your life and when it is time to do that there's not even enough money for you to live off of. Now you have to go find a job at seventy years old. Tell me how that's called living the

American dream. But hey that's what's ninety-five percent of the other people that love to live that way. While the other five percent enjoying life and making money. We get a chance to see our kids grow up. They traveling and just relaxing not worrying. Back in the day black people couldn't even read so they really couldn't work. So they picked up trades so they make money.   They couldn't even read but they made it. College wasn't always around. Education wasn't always a requirement to get a job either. Have you ever thought about why the United States is the only country that doesn't have free education? In order to get a degree, it cost thousands. To actually get a job in that field that you went to school for and actually work in the field it's highly unlikely. Have you ever wondered why the government jobs gets paid twice as more for the same job title. Majority of the people who have two or three degrees aren't working in their field. They're doing something else either because they were under-qualified(Lack of training)Why in the world would I need more training if I just graduated from college three to eight years ago? If college isn't training, what is it for? Then you have overqualified. How can you be overqualified for a job when you meet all the requirements needed for the job? In other words that can't pay you your worth? So if you got Education and Training and still can't get a job, doesn't it seem strange to you or are you like the ninety-five percent and believe you have to have a job. So you go work at a clothing

store or fast food
restaurant just to make
ends meet. It be the ones
that always have an
attitude. No one told you
to be a close minded
individual and just feels
like there's nothing
else. Honestly, a lot of
people feel like there is
nothing more because they
wasn't shown or taught
anything different.That's
completely
understandable. But when
will you start thinking
for you? Sometimes you

have to see what's out there for yourself. It's three kind of jobs out here. Commission,you control how much money you make. Base pay, they pay you how much they feel like your worth and they are in control of your life. Then you have salary. Basically, you can get paid whether you work or not. But anything over your set hours, basically you working for free. People seem to stay away from commission jobs. Sometimes you make no money if the product or service isn't sold. That is absolutely true. However, the money you make should be more than enough to take care of your bills. So when the no money days come in it shouldn't be an issue. Majority of the people who work commission jobs turns out to be business owners, bosses,the one with the most money.

  With commission pay jobs no taxes are taken out.

At the end of the year you get a 1099 form. Then you have to pay taxes. You only pay ten percent of what you made for the year. You get to write off things like getting your hair done or cut, your light bill, your rent depending on those percentage that you use for the job and so much more. Base pay jobs taxes are taken out. Two or four times a month depending on how many times you get paid.

Overtime it's just the money that they took away in taxes. News flash all the people that think that getting the bag by working to three jobs!!!!!!! You just becoming a slave to time and putting more strain on your body. The real definition of getting the bag is doing an hour or two of work and making 500 to $1,000 off of one product/ service. Then have the rest of the day actually live. The only way to really get the bag is control how much money you make and how you balance time.

Starting a business requires a lot of things but some of those things can come along the way and you can get them as you complete your journey of starting your own business. My very favorite thing to say so people is you have to start with what you have and advertise.

How to start a daycare

business

To get a home daycare
started. It's pretty
simple first. You do need
a place where you can
watch the children if you
have a two-story home.
You can use downstairs as
your facility. If you're
looking to get license
first you need to get put
on the list to take a
four hour class. Once you
take the four hour class
and get a certificate

you're free to continue from where you started after using your downstairs as of the facility. You will need a name for your business and it has to be registered with the Secretary of State. If you are in Tennessee Google Secretary of State, Tennessee. Once you Google you will see the price it is to register your business. You will also need business license. So

Google, where do you get a business license and find out the cost? Then you need to apply for an EIN number. Which means an employer identification number. You can only get two per social security number. So if you're going to use it for multiple businesses you might want to get one in your first and last name. When you register your business, you can always register as a DBA which means doing business as whatever you choose what your name to be? To apply for EIN it is free of charge. So if you pay for it, you did something wrong. To apply for EIN you go to irs.gov/businesses/small-businesses-self-employed/apply-for-an-employer-identification number /ein online.

If you are trying to be tax-exempt, make sure

your business is fully register and have all ducks in a row. In order to find children to watch you can go to care.com and place a listing. You can go to Craigslist and post a listing about watching kids. You can also place an ad in the Commercial Appeal. It's $5 for 14 days online with the commercial appeal.I believe to post on Craigslist its $5 for 45 days If I'm not mistaken. You can build a website.You can also advertise in Facebook groups. You may want to start working on your business credit as well. The best advertisement is word-of-mouth. So tell your families and friends. Promote yourself.I say do that for every business not just childcare. Start with what you have for every business. If you stay in apartment, you can start watching children. In Tennessee you can watch up to six kids without a license not including your own children. After a while You may want to get licensed. You will need a house building or someone can rent a center for community room. When it comes unlicensed make sure you call your local Department of Human Services Department for child care licensing to see how much they are paying per age bracket. Meaning see how much they would charge for a newborn to three years old;three to four years old;school age and how much they are charging for after school care. Or however, they have it setup. Make sure you call them to find it out. Also, check out the daycares around you. Check out your competition to make sure your price is unbeatable. If a parent has two or more children offer a discount.Also, make sure you add all your bills up to see how much you need to make a month then multiply that by four to see how much you need to make in the week then divide that by six to get an average of what you need to charge per child. Now being unlicensed you can get on the food program, but that requires them to be in and out your facility. For more information on that Google food programs for child care in my area. Now when watching other people's children, you got to be serious and act as if they're your own. In which they are because you'll be teaching,nourishing, and feeding them like your own. You may want to look into get into the TECTA program. Google it To see if it's available in your area. The more certifications you have the more people will take you serious and refer people to you.

If you're going to watch
the children, you should
provide two prices one
with Food and one
without. Please,keep in
mind affordability plus
being reasonable. Make
sure you are comfortable
with your hours of
operation. You can work
around parents schedule.
I can tell you that
requires dedication and
they expect for you to

stick with your hours. Be sure to have the fee in writing for late charge fee. Always always get a payment up front. I always give and get receipts. Please keep everything professional and you will gain respect. Be firm with the parents and the kids. As far as decoration goes you can find everything at Dollar Tree for starting off. Make sure you keep all receipts for tax purposes. If you make under $600 a year, you do not have to report your income. But if you make over $600 a year, you have to report your income. Every year you have to file taxes either using your business license or EIN number. If income is zero, file taxes to get a paper trail your business license or EIN number. You can get most of your things from Walmart and the parents bring towels and extra clothes. Check

out the thrift stores and
other places as time goes
on with your business.
I'm a firm believer in
starting with what you
got. So once you start
God will start on the
rest.